D1123444

Nature's Children

NEW WORLD MONKEYS

Amanda Harman

GROLIER
EDUCATIONAL

WOODLAND PUBLIC LIBRARY

FACTS IN BRIEF

Classification of New World monkeys

Class: *Mammalia* (mammals)

Order: *Primates* (people, apes, monkeys, and lemurs)

Family: *Callitrichidae* (marmosets and tamarins) and *Cebidae* (capuchin-like monkeys)

Genus: There are 16 genera of New World monkeys.

Species: There are 51 species of New World monkeys.

World distribution.   South and Central America.

Habitat.   Tropical rain forests.

Distinctive physical characteristics.   All New World monkeys have a broad nose with widely spaced nostrils. Most species have grasping hands and feet and a long, flexible tail.

Habits.   Active during the day and spend their life in trees. Some are very sociable, living in groups of up to 50 animals.

Diet.   Leaves, fruit, nuts, nectar, or tree sap, depending on the species. Many species feed on birds' eggs and insects, and some even catch and eat small animals such as frogs and small birds.

All rights reserved. Except for use in a review, no part of this book may be reproduced, stored in a retrieval system, or transmitted in any form, or by any means, electronic, mechanical photocopying, recording, or otherwise, without prior permission of the publisher.

© 1999 Brown Partworks Limited
Printed and bound in U.S.A.
Editor: James Kinchen
Designer: Tim Brown
Reprinted in 2002

Published by:

GROLIER
EDUCATIONAL

Sherman Turnpike, Danbury, Connecticut 06816

Library of Congress Cataloging-in-Publishing Data

New World Monkeys.
    p. cm. -- (Nature's children. Set 7)
   ISBN 0-7172-5540-9 (alk. paper) -- ISBN 0-7172-5531-X (set)
  1. New World Monkeys--Juvenile Literature. [1. New World Monkeys.] I. Grolier Educational (Firm) II. Series.

QL737.P925 N47 2001
599.8'5--dc21
                                           00-067253

Contents

Has your mom or dad ever called you a "little monkey"? If they have, the chances are you were getting up to mischief at the time! Monkeys are intelligent and lively creatures. They have a reputation for being playful and naughty, always doing things they should not be doing. Monkeys are also very noisy, and their chattering and "singing" fill their forest homes with sound.

There are lots of types of monkeys in the world, and they all look and act very differently. Sadly, people do not always treat these delightful creatures well, and they are among the most endangered animals on the planet. Read on in this book to learn all about these colorful animals and why we are in danger of losing them forever.

Opposite page:
This is a family of saki monkeys. These monkeys are famous for their huge, bushy tails.

Hairy Cousins

Opposite page: *This capuchin monkey is standing up because he is on lookout duty. When they stand like this, it is easy to see that New World monkeys are related to humans.*

Monkeys belong to the group of animals called the primates. The primates are members of the much larger group of animals called mammals. Like most mammals, primates have hairy skin, and the mothers feed their babies with milk from their own bodies. Other primates include lemurs, apes (gibbons, chimpanzees, orangutans, and gorillas), and even humans. How does it feel to know that you not only act like a little monkey sometimes, but are also closely related to one, too?

There are around 133 species (types) of monkeys, which scientists divide into two main groups. They are the Old World monkeys, which include the baboons and macaques, and the New World monkeys, which include the squirrel monkeys and the marmosets.

So if you go to a zoo and see a monkey, how can you tell whether it is a New World monkey or an Old World monkey? There are several ways to do this, as we shall see.

Noses and Bottoms

First, have a close look at the monkey's face. Does it have a broad nose with nostrils that are wide apart and point out to the sides? If so, it is a New World monkey. Old World monkeys have a narrower nose with nostrils that are close together and point down to the ground. If you are able to look inside the monkey's mouth, you should look to see whether or not it has cheek pouches for holding food. Some Old World monkeys have them, but New World monkeys do not.

Now have a look at its rear end. There is a good scientific reason for this, so try not to be too embarrassed! Old World monkeys often have large patches of hard skin on their bottoms. The patches protect the monkeys' rear ends when they are sitting down on the ground. New World monkeys do not have these useful cushions.

Opposite page: *This is a Goeldi's marmoset. Can you spot what it is about this monkey's face that lets you know that it is a New World monkey?*

Hands and Tails

Opposite page:
This squirrel monkey is using its opposable big toes to help it hold onto the branch. Although squirrel monkeys have a long tail, they cannot use it to hold onto things.

If you are still not sure whether your monkey is a New World monkey or an Old World monkey, take a look at its hands. Many Old World monkeys have thumbs that can be held opposite their fingers. That lets them use their hands to pick things up, just as you can. Thumbs that work like this are called opposable thumbs. Most New World monkeys do not have these opposable thumbs. Like Old World monkeys, however, they do have opposable big toes on their feet.

Another thing that will help you decide is the monkey's tail. What many New World monkeys have that Old World monkeys do not is a long, flexible tail that can be used to grasp things with. This tail probably makes up for their lack of opposable thumbs!

Where on Earth?

Old World monkeys and New World monkeys are found in different places around the world. Old World monkeys live in Asia and Africa, while New World monkeys live in Central and South America.

All New World monkeys live in warm, tropical forests. Some prefer wet woodlands on low, swampy ground, while others live higher up in rain forests. One thing all these monkeys agree on, however, is that they like life best up in the trees.

Opposite page: *This golden-headed tamarin lives in the forests of southern Brazil.*

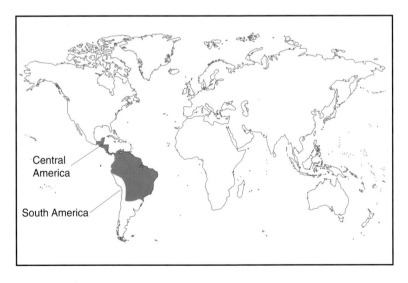

Central
America

South America

The area shaded brown on this map shows the places where New World monkeys live.

Comical Faces

Opposite page:
This is an emperor tamarin. These monkeys are named for their large white mustaches, which make them look like the 19th-century German emperor Kaiser Wilhelm I.

The many species of New World monkeys look very different from each other. Some species have short, thick fur colored gray, black, or brown. In other species the fur has brightly colored patterns in reds, yellows, and white. These patterns can often make a monkey's face look very cute or comical. For example, the squirrel monkey has a funny little face, with a dark head and muzzle, white ears and chin, and a white mask around its eyes.

Other New World monkeys have long, silky fur. They are the marmosets and tamarins. Some of these little monkeys also have long, drooping mustaches, big tufts on their ears, or large wiglike manes and crests on their heads. The lion tamarin gets its name because it has a beautiful golden mane and looks just like a miniature lion.

The Big and the Small

New World monkeys also come in a many different sizes. The largest New World monkey is the woolly spider monkey. It is also known as the *muriqui* by the people who live in its Brazilian home. The woolly spider monkey has a long body and legs, and can weigh more than 26 pounds (12 kilograms). The tail of this monkey is even longer than its body, measuring as many as 29 inches (74 centimeters) in length. This animal is the New World monkey that looks most like its ape cousins, such as the gibbons and chimpanzees.

The smallest New World monkey is the pygmy marmoset. It weighs no more than 7 ounces (190 grams). If you saw this tiny animal, you might not believe it was a monkey at all. It looks just like a miniature cat or a rodent such as a squirrel!

Opposite page:
Pygmy marmosets are the smallest monkeys in the world. They usually make holes in trees and feed on the sap and gum that leak out. Sometimes, though, they may eat fruit as this one is doing.

Getting Around

Opposite page:
Spider monkeys got their name because their long arms and legs make them look like big, hairy spiders! They are better at getting around in the trees than almost any of the other monkeys.

Unlike many Old World monkeys, all New World monkeys spend their life in the trees. Many of them never leave the branches. One or two species do occasionally climb down to the forest floor to play with each other or to find food, however. Woolly monkeys can even stand up and walk on their hind legs.

Monkeys travel through their leafy home in lots of different ways. You can often tell how a monkey gets around by looking at the shape of its body. Some monkeys are very small and have claws on their fingers and toes. The claws help them scurry along branches and scamper up tree trunks like squirrels. Others have powerful hind legs and can leap large distances from tree to tree, using their tails to help them balance in the air. One kind of monkey—the uakari—is the only New World monkey to have a short tail. It climbs among the branches but rarely jumps very far.

Swinging Acrobats

Opposite page:
Spider monkeys have the longest and most powerful tails of any monkey.

Some large New World monkeys have long arms. They use them for swinging from tree to tree, like acrobats in a circus. These animals have hands shaped like large hooks to help them do this. They also have long tails, which look just like a fifth limb. This tail has powerful muscles and is so strong that the monkeys can use it to grab hold of a branch. The monkeys can then hang with their hands and feet free for feeding or cleaning themselves.

The tail is also very sensitive and can be used to touch things. Beneath the tip there is a bare patch of skin with lines on it that looks just like the prints on your fingers. This bare patch makes the tip of the tail very sensitive and good to grip things with. Some monkeys can even use their tails like an extra hand to pick up objects such as pieces of food.

Tasty Morsels

Nearly all New World monkeys sleep at night and are out and about during the day. A lot of their time is spent in collecting food. Some species are carnivores (meat-eaters) and hunt out animals such as small snakes, lizards, frogs, and baby birds. They also eat insects and spiders, and have long fingers for poking into holes in tree bark or among the leaves. Other monkeys prefer to eat nuts, birds' eggs, and the nectar from flowers. Marmosets have sharp, pointed teeth for gnawing tree bark so they can lick the sap underneath. Howler monkeys sometimes feed on nothing but leaves, and they spend a long time choosing the youngest and freshest morsels to eat. The favorite food of most New World monkeys, however, is fruit. The monkeys get especially excited whenever a fig tree produces ripe figs and will squabble noisily among themselves for the juicy fruit.

Hanging around Together

Like people, monkeys are very sociable creatures. All New World monkeys live in groups that are called troops—some are small family groups, while others are made up of a few adult males and several females with their babies. In some species a troop may contain as many as 50 monkeys. Generally, the troop will protect its own area of forest against other monkey groups. This area is their territory.

Many animals gather in groups to make each other feel safe from predators (animals that eat them). Monkeys have few enemies that can reach them in the trees, however. They probably hang around together so that they can defend their territory from intruders. It also means they can chase away other monkeys from the fruit trees that carry their favorite food. The owl, or night, monkey does not need to do this so much, because it only comes out to feed at night, when all the other monkeys are in bed. For this reason its troops are quite small, containing only about five animals.

Noisy Chatter

If you were to wander through a South American rain forest in the daytime, you would probably hear the monkeys even before you saw them. That is because these animals like to chatter and call out to tell each other things, just like us. Some monkeys have squeaky voices and sing and twitter just like birds. Monkeys use noises to scare away intruders, to let each other know where they are, to warn each other about a predator, and to call the troop to feed.

Howler monkeys are particularly well known for their voices. They get their name because they gather in groups in the morning and the evening, and howl as loud as they can. These calls can be heard through the forest several miles away. The calls warn other howler monkeys to keep out of the troop's territory. A howler monkey's howl is one of the loudest sounds made by any animal on Earth!

Opposite page:
Howler monkeys have special inflatable sacs in their throats that make their calls even louder.

Keeping in Touch

Opposite page:
These woolly spider monkeys are having a "group hug" in this tree!

We have seen how important sound is to New World monkeys, but hearing is not the only sense these animals use to communicate with each other. Sight is important, too. Many monkeys make faces or stick up their ear tufts or other fur to show how they are feeling. The bald uakari has a bare face that turns different shades of red, depending on what it wants to say. The marmosets and tamarins also "talk" to each other using scent. They chew the tree bark with their sharp teeth to soften the wood. Then they pee on the soft wood to mark it with their scent.

One of the main senses in a monkey's life, however, is touch. The members of a monkey troop spend a lot of time cleaning and looking after each other's fur. This grooming not only keeps the monkeys' fur clean but also helps keep their friendships close. Titi monkeys even twine their tails together when they are resting.

One Baby or Two?

New World monkeys are able to breed at any time of year. In many species all or most of the males and females in a troop mate with each other. In some monkey troops, however, only one female is allowed to breed at one time. Among these monkeys the other troop members help the parents bring up their offspring until the female can no longer breed. Then it becomes a different female's turn. Titi monkeys are unusual because each has only one mating partner, with whom it stays all its life.

Most New World monkeys mate once a year and give birth to one baby at a time. Marmosets and tamarins usually have twins each time they give birth, however. These monkeys also have a short pregnancy of about four months, so they are able to have two sets of twins every year. This makes them very fast breeders compared to other monkeys.

Opposite page: *If they have a good life, these young marmosets on their parent's back may live to be more than 10 years old.*

Taking Care of Baby

Opposite page: *This baby emperor tamarin is still too young to have a long mustache like its parent.*

When they are born, baby monkeys are already covered with fur and have their eyes open. They cling tightly to their mother's belly or back right away. The mother will carry her little one around with her for the first few weeks of its life, until it is strong enough to move around the trees on its own. Mom will continue to feed her baby with milk for a few months. Common woolly monkeys feed their young with milk for a whole year.

In titi monkeys the father carries the baby most of the time. Among marmosets and tamarins the father helps to take care of his offspring, too. In these monkeys the baby's older brothers and sisters also take turns in carrying the little monkey while its mother feeds herself. Night monkeys stay in their family groups until they are about two and a half years old. During this time they help take care of their young brothers and sisters. Doing this probably helps the youngsters when they are parents themselves.

Capuchins usually only give birth to one baby.
So, these two youngsters are probably just friends.

Playing like Monkeys

Young monkeys are playful little animals and love nothing better than to chase each other and get into play fights. Some monkeys also like to sit and play around with things like leaves, twigs, and stones. Although all this play looks like great fun, the youngsters are actually doing something very serious. They are learning all the skills they will need in later life—skills that they will use to find or catch their food or run away from their enemies. The young monkeys also learn how to get along with the other members of their troop. That is especially useful for when they get older and start to look for a mate.

Among some monkeys the males leave the troop in which they were born as soon as they become old enough to have babies of their own. In others the offspring stay in their original family group for the rest of their life.

Pretty Monkeys

Opposite page: *This beautiful monkey is a cotton-top tamarin. These monkeys live in Colombia in South America.*

Scientists divide the New World monkeys up into two families. The first family contains the tiny, silken-haired marmosets and tamarins. There are 21 species in this family, and they live in the tropical forests of Brazil, Bolivia, Peru, Colombia, and Ecuador. They all look very different from each other. Many are brightly colored, and lots have manes or tufts of hair over their ears, on top of their head, or hanging down from their faces. These tufts make the marmosets and tamarins very easy to recognize. The cotton-top tamarin is particularly striking, with a shock of long, white hair like an aging rock star.

Some scientists consider the Goeldi's monkey to belong to the marmoset and tamarin family, too. This dark little creature had not been described before 1904, and it is the most recent primate to have been discovered.

Howling Vegetarians

The second New World monkey family contains around 30 species. They are divided up into several smaller groups. They are the howler monkeys, the spider monkeys and woolly monkeys, the uakaris and sakis, the capuchins, the titi monkeys, and the night and squirrel monkeys.

There are around six species of howlers, and they are all big monkeys. Some male black howler monkeys weigh as much as 17 and a half pounds (8 kilograms)—that's as heavy as a fully grown labrador dog. Being so big, howler monkeys need to spend a lot of time eating their favorite food—leaves. Leaves are not very satisfying, however, so the howler monkeys also eat insects, flowers, nuts, and fruit. These monkeys live high in the forest canopy in groups of several females and their young, with a male that is in charge. Males that do not have their own troop will fight to take over ones belonging to other males.

Opposite page:
Howler monkeys have special bacteria in their stomach that help them break down leaves after they have swallowed them.

Big Monkeys, Big Brains

Opposite page:
A white-faced capuchin monkey. Capuchin monkeys are some of the cleverest monkeys and can be trained to do many different things.

When you think of a monkey, the picture you bring up in your mind is probably that of a spider monkey. Spider monkeys are not only the biggest and the most acrobatic monkeys in the New World—they also may be the most intelligent. Scientists have found that they have the biggest brains compared to their body size of all the South and Central American monkeys. Woolly monkeys are closely related to spider monkeys, and they move through the trees in much the same way as their cousins. These monkeys get their name because of their short, thick fur.

Spider monkeys and woolly monkeys are unusual among the New World monkeys because their troops do not stay the same all the time. Members of the group come and go every day. The groups are largest whenever there is a lot of food, such as fruit, in a small area in the forest.

Bald Monkeys

With its short tail, shaggy white or reddish fur, and naked face with bright red skin, the bald uakari is instantly recognizable. This monkey likes to live high in the trees in low-lying swampy forests in Brazil, Colombia, and Peru. The black-headed uakari does not look as strange as its bald-faced cousin. It has a dark face and reddish brown hair, and it looks much like a spider monkey, but without the long, grasping tail.

Sakis and bearded sakis are close relatives of the uakaris. These animals have strong teeth that let them eat the seeds they find inside pieces of fruit. They never have a problem with other monkeys stealing their food, because other monkeys cannot eat these seeds. There are four species of saki monkeys and two species of bearded sakis. Male and female Guianan sakis are easy to tell apart because males have a white face, while females do not.

Opposite page: *This colorful monkey is a bald uakari. If they cannot find enough food to eat in the trees, these monkeys will come down to the ground to look for seeds.*

A Mixed Bag

Opposite page:
A night monkey's huge eyes help it see when it is looking for food during the night.

The last members of the New World monkeys are the squirrel monkeys, the capuchins, the titi monkeys, and the night monkey. The night monkey gets its name because it comes out to feed at night—in fact, it is the only monkey in the world that is active at night. This unusual creature is also known as the owl monkey. That's because young males travel through the forest around the time of the full moon, making loud hooting noises to attract females. Their faces also look a little like those of owls because of the rings of colored fur around their huge eyes.

All these monkeys are relatively small. The smallest of all of them are the squirrel monkeys, which grow no more than 14 and a half inches (37 centimeters) long from their head to their rump. They have a long, slender tail. Squirrel monkeys gather in large, noisy groups, scampering playfully along branches and leaping among the trees.

New World Monkeys and People

The New World monkeys are such funny animals, and they are so noisy and colorful, that the world would be a sadder place without them. Unfortunately, the lives of many of them are in danger. All these animals are at risk from losing their homes. That is because people are cutting down the tropical forests where they live to make way for buildings, roads, and farmland. Most New World monkeys have also been caught in huge numbers for food and so that they can be kept as pets or in zoos. Many marmoset and tamarin monkeys were also killed because people thought that they carried diseases such as yellow fever and malaria.

Of all the New World Monkeys the lion tamarins and woolly spider monkeys are in the most danger. There are fewer than 1,000 black lion tamarins left in the wild. They live in such a small area that these monkeys could become extinct at any time. The woolly spider monkey is in even more danger since there are probably fewer than 300 alive in the wild today.

Words to Know

Ape The group of primates that do not have a tail and are cleverer than other primates, apart from humans.

Breed To produce young.

Carnivore An animal that eats other animals.

Endangered When an animal is in danger of becoming extinct.

Extinct When all of the animals of a particular species have died, and there are no more left anywhere in the world.

Grooming To clean or brush, especially hair or fur.

Mammal Any warm-blooded animal that gives birth to live young and produces milk to feed them.

Mate To come together to produce young.

Opposable thumb A thumb that can be held opposite the fingers so the hand can be used to easily pick up objects.

Predator An animal that hunts other animals (prey) for food.

Primate The group of mammals that includes monkeys, lemurs, apes, and humans.

Species A particular type of animal.

Territory An area where an animal hunts or breeds. The animal generally defends its territory against other animals.

Troop A group of monkeys.

INDEX

Cover Photo: Haroldo Palo Jr. / NHPA
Photo Credits: Jany Sauvanet / NHPA, pages 4, 11, 34, 42; Gerad Lacz / NHPA, page 7; Rod Williams / Bruce Coleman, pages 8, 30; Haroldo Palo Jr. / NHPA, page 12; Martin Harvey / NHPA, page 15; Bruce Coleman, pages 16, 26; Staffan Widstrand / Bruce Coleman, page 19; Kevin Schafer / NHPA, pages 21, 24, 29, 33; Stephen Dalton / NHPA, pages 37, 45; James Carmichael Jr. / NHPA, page 38; Daniel Heuclin / NHPA, page 41.